LOVE YOUR
ENEMY

LOVE YOUR
ENEMY

Oluseye S. Olayiwola

Copyright © 2024 by Oluseye S. Olayiwola

No part of this publication may be reproduced, stored in a retrieval system, or transmitted, in any form or by any means – electronic, mechanical, photocopying, recording, or otherwise – without prior written permission.

All scripture quotations are taken from the New King James Version. ©1982 by Thomas Nelson, Inc. Used by permission. All rights reserved.

ISBN: 979-834-62903-6-0

Published by:

PenPixel Digital Press

Phone/WhatsApp: +447925171979
Website: www.penpixeldp.com

Email: info@penpixeldp.com/penpixeldp@gmail.com

I dedicate this book to everyone that believes that loving one's enemy is not as hard as it seems.

CONTENTS

Introduction   7

Chapter One
Your Enemy   8

Chapter Two
You Can Be Someone's Enemy   18

Chapter Three
Love Your Enemy (I)   26

Chapter Four
Love Your Enemy (II)   43

Chapter Five
Yes, You Can   61

INTRODUCTION

Love is who God is. Anyone that is in God's image is expected to be full of love too. In other words, love is meant to be who we are if we believe that God is our Father. Therefore, loving our enemies should be because it is in our nature to love.

CHAPTER ONE

YOUR ENEMY

Love Your Enemy

I would like to start by defining an enemy as someone that ultimately seeks to do you harm/evil because they hate you or love themselves more. 'Ultimately' here talks of those that come to you as friends or someone that cares for you but later do you harm, because it was in their intention from the start to harm you, or the reason they became your friend or care for you in the first place is to harm you.

We need to first establish the basic reason your enemy is your enemy. This reason is the fact that they hate you or love themselves more. Therefore, anyone that hates you is automatically your enemy, or anyone that loves themself more than you will automatically do things that will harm you. It is not just what someone does to you that makes them your enemy, but the fact that they hate you. Although hatred is not the same

Your Enemy

as loving oneself more, but these two conditions will cause someone to harm another person.

So bearing in mind that the fundamental ingredient for someone to be your enemy is hatred or loving themselves more than you, we will look at some other reasons why anyone can be your enemy.

- ***They are your enemies because they think you have what they want or what is theirs, or because you actually have what is theirs.***

Simply because they believe that they are the ones that should have what you have, they begin to hate you and wish you evil, such that when they are in a position to carry out that evil on you, they will. A good example of this is when a poor person hates a rich person just because he is rich. Furthermore, if you have in your possession what actually belongs to them, even if it is possible to be with such things unknowingly, they can hate you for this and thereby have a supposed legal backing to harm you or act wickedly towards you.

• ***They are your enemies because they have the power to be so, or power to do whatever they want.***
Power can be easily intoxicating, especially when it is of great magnitude or potency. Therefore, your enemy uses their power against you simply because they can, that is why they can do evil or act wickedly towards you for very silly or unreasonable reasons. For example, some people who are into witchcraft (as Nigerians know witchcraft) can say because you did not greet them, or you greeted them in a particular way, they will make you go mad. Isn't this too

Your Enemy

much? They do it simply because they have the power to do such.

Another example could be someone giving you a condition that is not official or legal before you get a thing that you are qualified for, just because they are the one in the position to release it to you. It could even be that you are not qualified for it, and instead of letting you go, they give it to you to use it against you later, or blackmail you, or to make you do what you should not.

- ***They are your enemies because they believe that they are right, or because they are actually right.***

They hate you because they believe that they are right and you are wrong, and you do not want to accept that they are right. In this case they

Love Your Enemy

may actually be wrong, but as long as they still believe they are right, they will oppose you.

But in the case where they are actually right and you are wrong, they can still hate you for not accepting that they are right, and so do anything, most times, wicked or harmful things to show or prove to you that they are right.

It is also possible that you are both right, that is, they are right and you are also right, but because they want their own way to be done, and/or because you are not accepting their being right, they can do harmful things to you to prove their point.

There are a few points I would like us to note about the enemy:

Your Enemy

- ***The enemy cannot influence the entire world against you.***

Your enemy, no matter how strong or influential, cannot influence the entire world against you. One reason for this is that their power and influence is limited. Therefore, you do not need to be afraid of them. If you are hard working and skillful, you will definitely get an opportunity where their influence cannot reach and thrive there. Even if your enemy is fetish or has *juju*, the influence or power of their *juju* cannot affect the entire world, but what they usually do is to place a curse on you, so that it will follow you wherever you go, thereby making it appear like the entire world is against you. Therefore, if whatever

> *Your enemy, no matter how strong or influential, cannot influence the entire world against you.*

Love Your Enemy

they do against you cannot stick to you or stick with you, you will never be under the influence of their wickedness. But you need to know how to ensure that it will not stick to you. And the power of God is able to break every curse.

- ***The enemy can only use power, truth or lies against you.***

You need to understand that the enemy can only use power, truth or lies against you. That is all they can use. Power usually is no respecter of anything except higher or greater power. When your enemy realizes that their power is more than yours, they can oppress you. Or when you are ignorant of the fact that you have more power than them, they can oppress you simply because they have the power to do so.

Your Enemy

Truth is the other tool that your enemy uses against you. A lot of enemies use truth because most of them do not actually have any power. For example, if you always arrive late to work and the records says so, a wicked boss or any other person can use this against you because it is true that you arrive late to work. Or, if you are occupying someone else's land, knowingly or unknowingly, the rightful owner of the land can do with you as they please, because it is true that the land belongs to them. There is no greater weapon in the hands of your enemy than the truth but thank God that even the lawful captive can be delivered.

Lies or deception is the least on this list. When the enemy knows that they cannot use power and/or truth against you, the next thing they resort to is to lie against you and/or try to deceive you

Love Your Enemy

into doing something that will become a snare to you. They have no other tool to use against you other than these three. Or we can put it this way: whatever the enemy is using against you can be categorized under power, truth, and lies.

The reason I am pointing this out is that anyone that is in Christ has the solutions to them in Jesus.

Please note that the enemy we are talking about here are human beings that hate you and want to do you harm, not the devil and demons or spiritual wickedness.

Chapter Two

YOU CAN BE SOMEONE'S ENEMY

Love Your Enemy

From the definition of enemy earlier, an enemy is someone that ultimately seeks or wants to do harm/evil to someone else because of hatred or loving themself more. And I also emphasized that the main ingredient for being an enemy is hatred or loving yourself more.

Therefore, if you hate anyone, or love yourself more than such a one, you are automatically that person's enemy. But you might say that I do not want to harm anyone or do evil to anyone despite the fact that I hate them. What you do not know is that the only inspiration that can come out of hatred is evil, or the only product of loving yourself more is wickedness on others. You cannot wish good out of hatred. That is why you may not know you are wishing evil when you hate someone until the deed is done, or when you rejoice when evil happens to them.

You Can Be Someone's Enemy

Hatred leads to evil, therefore, if you truly do not want to harm anyone or do evil to them, do not allow hatred in your heart. No matter how genuine the reason is, do not allow the tiniest bit of hatred in your heart.

> *You cannot wish good out of hatred.*

The other aspect is the 'loving yourself more' part. Let us look at it: in the scriptures, we were told that we are to love our neighbor as ourselves. Not more than ourselves, or less than ourselves, but as ourselves. Love is experienced at its fullest when it is expressed on a plane or at the same level. You may have a greater magnitude of love in you to give but you must be at the same plane with whomsoever you want to give it to, little wonder we grow in God's love. If you love yourself more than anyone, you will definitely

Love Your Enemy

do things that will hurt the person, or you will definitely do things that will not be good to the person, especially when you have a consideration to make between you and the person. Loving yourself more will make you partial and cause you to despise the other person. Although what you can do to others because you love yourself more may not be as grave as what you can do if you hate them, but its effect on the heart is almost the same, so they are both birds of a feather.

Let me explain a little what I mean by the effect on the heart is the same.

When you hate someone, you wish them evil or bad luck, and when a good opportunity presents itself, you do this evil to them. If they do not hate you for what you have done to them, at least

You Can Be Someone's Enemy

they will not be happy with you. Similarly, if you love yourself more than someone, you will want to ensure that you get the best or you satisfy yourself first at the expense of such a person, or not being mindful of how it will affect the person. When you do this, that person will not be happy with you for treating them that way if they do not hate you in return. Although hatred will cause you to bring far greater pain and/or bodily harm to someone than 'loving yourself more' but no one will be happy with receiving the outcome of either of them.

Furthermore, I have discovered that a lot of times, those that we believe are our enemies are truly not so, because we came to this conclusion based on what they did or what they are doing but not by trying to see if they hate us or not. Action is not enough to conclude on who a

Love Your Enemy

person truly is, you need to add intention or motive. Yes, an action can be categorized as good or bad, and truly so, but a personality cannot be known on this alone but also by motive or intention. Therefore, a lot of patience is needed when drawing conclusions on who a person is. You also need the help of the Holy Spirit to know anyone. In fact, it is only the Holy Spirit that can help you truly know anyone. You cannot conclude that anyone is your enemy just by one act of wickedness or evil, you have to look beyond the act to see if there is hatred in the person's heart towards you. A lot of times, people do wicked/evil things to us unknowingly or unintentionally, and so this does not make them our enemy.

> *It is only the Holy Spirit that can help you truly know anyone.*

You Can Be Someone's Enemy

In addition, even if someone has acted wickedly to you several or countless times, you still need to look for the hatred part before concluding that the person is your enemy.

ASSUMED ENEMIES	REAL ENEMIES
Do not hate you.	Hate you.
Harm you unknowingly or unintentionally.	Harm you purposefully.
They are against you unknowingly or unintentionally.	They work against you intentionally.

People that hate you usually do not hide it except they are your subordinate. But those that do not hate you can harm you unknowingly or as a result of responding to life threatening actions from you. When people are threatened, or feel threatened, they can do anything to help themselves, so if you happen to be on the

Love Your Enemy

receiving end, it will appear like they are your enemy.

I believe that it may not be easy to wait to know if someone hates you or not irrespective of their actions, but the main issue is that you must not allow hatred to have a hold on your heart for anyone no matter what they have done to you, or what they are doing to you. You are permitted to hate things and/or circumstances, but do not hate people.

Action is not enough to conclude on who a person truly is, you need to add intention or motive.

CHAPTER THREE

LOVE YOUR ENEMY (I)

Love Your Enemy

"You have heard that it was said, 'You shall love your neighbor and hate your enemy.' But I say to you, love your enemies, bless those who curse you, do good to those who hate you, and pray for those who spitefully use you and persecute you, that you may be sons of your Father in heaven; for He makes His sun rise on the evil and on the good, and sends rain on the just and on the unjust. For if you love those who love you, what reward have you? Do not even the tax collectors do the same? And if you greet your brethren only, what do you do more than others? Do not even the tax collectors do so? Therefore you shall be perfect, just as your Father in heaven is perfect.

(Matthew 5:43-48)

(You can also read Luke 6:27-36)

Love Your Enemy (I)

To love your enemy is not as hard as it seems. You simply need to have the right nature, which is only possible in Christ Jesus. It is one thing to do something because you have been promised a reward; it is another thing to do it because it is in your nature to do so. A lot of people are pious or moral because they are expecting a reward or hope that their good deeds will speak for them one day. As good as this can be, it is nothing compared to having the nature of God in Christ Jesus in you. As we saw in Jesus' words in verse forty-eight above that when we love our enemies, we exhibit the nature of our heavenly Father, this is the primary reason for loving our enemies. Especially for anyone that is in Christ, love is your nature, love is who you are, because love is who your heavenly Father is.

Love Your Enemy

Beloved, let us love one another, for love is of God; and everyone who loves is born of God and knows God. He who does not love does not know God, for God is love.

(1 John 4:7-8)

When something is your nature, it does not matter what is done to you, that is what will come out of you. For example, it is in a dog's nature to bark, no matter what language you speak to the dog, it will bark back at you. It is not possible for the dog to speak back to you in your own language just because you have trained it, but it can bark back at you in a way that responds to the training you have given it. Similarly, love is

> *To love your enemy is not as hard as it seems. You simply need to have the right nature.*

Love Your Enemy (I)

meant to be our nature such that no matter what is done to us, it is only love that we will give in return, in other words, no matter the wickedness done to us, it is only good that we will do in return, because it is in our nature to do good.

Love is of the Spirit while hatred is of the flesh.

> ***Now the works of the flesh are evident, which are: adultery, fornication, uncleanness, lewdness, idolatry, sorcery, hatred, contentions, jealousies, outbursts of wrath, selfish ambitions, dissensions, heresies.***
> **(Galatians 5:19-20)**

Love Your Enemy

But the fruit of the Spirit is love, joy, peace, longsuffering, kindness, goodness, faithfulness.
(Galatians 5:22)

Every time you act in love you prove that you are not just a bundle of emotions, responding to feelings and physical stimulus; you are much more than what your body says or responds to. You are indeed a Spirit, you have a Soul, and you live through a Body. You are not controlled by your flesh—what your body says or craves. When you have the life of Christ in you, Jesus is your Lord and King; you are indeed alive in your spirit. Your spirit is in charge. Therefore, love is who you are, and love is all you give. I know that you might say that we are still in this world, and it is difficult to always walk in love. It will be difficult if you focus on the flesh, it is

Love Your Enemy (I)

not possible to look towards the west and see the east at the same time. Despite the fact that you are a spirit being, if you focus on the flesh that is what you will do. If you focus on the Spirit and crucify the flesh, you will walk in the Spirit, provided that you already have the life of Christ in you, that is, you are already born-again.

And those who are Christ's have crucified the flesh with its passions and desires. If we live in the Spirit, let us also walk in the Spirit.
(Galatians 5:24-25)

The primary way of loving your enemy is like a two-edged sword: we have seen one edge which is the fact that love is your nature, because you are of your heavenly Father; the other edge is to look unto God and not your enemy.

Love Your Enemy

If you focus on your enemy, it will be impossible to love them, because you will only see the wickedness they do to you, you will also see their hatred, so you will not be able to do anything else than to respond in like manner to them. But when you look up to God, you will not only see love, but you will also be able to learn from Him how to express His love perfectly. God does not want anything or anyone to be between you and Him.

God promised to be the one to take care of our enemies when we follow Him and make Him our total focus. In fact, when we truly follow Him, He will not only take care of our enemies, but He will also take care of everything that concerns us.

Love Your Enemy (I)

Let us see a few scriptures:

> *I will bless those who bless you, And I will curse him who curses you; And in you all the families of the earth shall be blessed."*
>
> **(Genesis 12:3)**

> *But if you indeed obey His voice and do all that I speak, then I will be an enemy to your enemies and an adversary to your adversaries. So you shall serve the LORD your God, and He will bless your bread and your water. And I will take sickness away from the midst of you. I will send My fear before you, I will cause confusion among all the people to whom you*

Love Your Enemy

come, and will make all your enemies turn their backs to you.

(Exodus 23:22,25,27)

"Now it shall come to pass, if you diligently obey the voice of the LORD your God, to observe carefully all His commandments which I command you today, that the LORD your God will set you high above all nations of the earth. And all these blessings shall come upon you and overtake you, because you obey the voice of the LORD your God...

"The LORD will cause your enemies who rise against you to be defeated before your face; they shall come out

Love Your Enemy (I)

against you one way and flee before you seven ways.
(Deuteronomy 28:1,2,7)

God promised to curse those that cursed Abram so that Abram does not need to concern himself with dealing with those that curse him.

God told the children of Israel that if they served and hearken to His voice, He would cause their enemies that comes before them one way to flee from them seven ways.

You cannot deal with your enemies better than the way God will deal with them. More so, you are extremely limited, and what you will use to judge your enemies is also limited, therefore, God is the best person to take care of your enemies. So rather than focus on how you can

Love Your Enemy

deal with your enemies, you need to focus on God: focus on knowing His ways; focus on growing in His love.

Dealing with your enemies yourself is a waste of time and effort. You will also miss the glorious things that God has for you in Him. There is so much to see and know in God that this one lifetime on earth is not enough, so wasting precious time that could have been used to grow in the knowledge of God to be concerned about your enemies should not be encouraged at all.

The truth is that when you grow in God, you will see that you do not actually have any enemy, because when God is with you, no one can be against you. When you are in God, and you know that you are, no one can harm you.

Love Your Enemy (I)

There is no darkness in light. Enemies are of darkness. You are a light, knowing who you are in God is the best way to deal with your enemies, not hating them in return. The more you grow in God the easier it becomes to love your enemies.

> *The more you grow in God the easier it becomes to love your enemies.*

So let me submit to you that if you have any enemy that is able to cause you to hate them, it is because you have drifted away from God. For you to remain in hatred for more than a moment means that you have disconnected from God.

I know that it is almost impossible not to feel hatred towards someone, but it should only be for a moment for anyone that is in Christ. You must not make hatred an abode.

Love Your Enemy

"The LORD is my shepherd; I shall not want."

"You prepare a table before me in the presence of my enemies; You anoint my head with oil; My cup runs over."
(Psalm 23:1, 5)

Here we see that when the LORD is your shepherd, you shall not want. He will prepare a table for you in the presence of your enemies. The main issue here is when the LORD is your shepherd. When you follow the LORD'S leading, your enemy will have to be able to stop the LORD before they can stop you. And we know that no one can stop the LORD or move Him.

Love Your Enemy (I)

When a man's way please the LORD, He makes even his enemies to be at peace with him.

(Proverbs 16:7)

Here we see again that the LORD must be your focus, not your enemies. And He makes your enemies to be at peace with you. When you live for God or in God, it is not your duty to deal with your enemies, God does that for you. You have no reason to hate your enemies, because they cannot harm you in God, and God takes care of them for you.

No weapon formed against you shall prosper, And every tongue which rises against you in judgment You shall condemn. This is the heritage of the servants of the LORD, And

Love Your Enemy

their righteousness is of Me," Says the LORD.

(Isaiah 54:17)

Here we see again that no weapon fashioned against you shall prosper because it is your heritage in the LORD. As long as you belong to the LORD, security is part of the benefits you enjoy.

Someone might say that, but God led Jesus to die at the hands of His enemies. Jesus did not die at the hands of His enemies because they overpowered Him, but because He laid His life down by Himself. He gave Himself to them so that He might through that death save the whole world, and more so, He resurrected.

Love Your Enemy (I)

"Therefore My Father loves Me, because I lay down My life that I may take it again.

"No one takes it from Me, but I lay it down of Myself. I have power to lay it down, and I have power to take it again. This command I have received from My Father."

(John 10:17-18)

In conclusion, when God is your focus, when He is the only one you receive all your supplies and directions from, no enemy can harm you or make your life miserable. Therefore, it will be easy for you to love your enemy indeed.

Chapter Four

LOVE YOUR ENEMY (II)

Love Your Enemy

"You have heard that it was said, 'You shall love your neighbor and hate your enemy.'

"But I say to you, love your enemies, bless those who curse you, do good to those who hate you, and pray for those who spitefully use you and persecute you,

(Matthew 5:43-44)

*I*t was Jesus that said that we should love our enemies; He is the one that brought light into this matter, taking us from being ordinary people to being divine just like our heavenly Father.

Jesus is the manifested, tangible expression of love (God). As He is the pioneer of 'loving our

Love Your Enemy (II)

enemies,' He is the best person to help you to do the same. Without Jesus, it is impossible to genuinely love your enemies.

We saw earlier that the key to loving your enemy is to look to God, and follow Him. The only way to God and to become like Him is Jesus Christ.

> ***Jesus said to him, "I am the way, the truth, and the life. No one comes to the Father except through me.***
>
> **(John 14:6)**

Jesus is the life; it is only through Him that you can have love as your nature. It is only through Him that love can be your essence. And it is only as you grow in Jesus that you also grow in love.

Love Your Enemy

"Abide in Me, and I in you. As the branch cannot bear fruit of itself, unless it abides in the vine, neither can you, unless you abide in Me.

(John 15:4)

But the fruit of the Spirit is love, joy, peace, longsuffering, kindness, goodness, faithfulness,

(Galatians 5:22)

When you accept Jesus into your heart and make Him Lord of every area of your life, you receive His life as your own such that the life you now live is Christ's, and you follow His leading in every area of your life, you will grow in His love and definitely find it easy to love your enemies.

Love Your Enemy (II)

Jesus is the truth. Therefore when you are in Him, and you grow in Him, you will also grow in truth through the help of the Holy Spirit.

> ***"However, when He, the Spirit of truth, has come, He will guide you into all truth; for He will not speak on His own authority, but whatever He hears He will speak; and He will tell you things to come.***
>
> **(John 16:13)**

The truth is that without the help of the Holy Spirit you cannot be guided into all truth, you will want to see the truth only from your own perspective, and thereby miss it totally.

Love Your Enemy

"He will glorify Me, for He will take of what is Mine and declare it to you. All things that the Father has are Mine. Therefore I said that He will take of Mine and declare it to you.
(John 16:14-15)

Jesus is the truth that you are growing in, as He said that the Spirit of truth will take of what is His and declare it to you. As you grow in Jesus, it becomes easier for you to walk in truth, speak the truth, be truthful in your dealings and interactions, until it becomes impossible for you to be otherwise.

Remember that we said that one category of what the enemy can use against you is truth or lies. Since you have become truthful in Christ, you will not want to do anything that will

Love Your Enemy (II)

become a snare to you, for example, you will not become a perpetual late comer to work. And if you mistakenly do anything that the enemy wants to use against you, the Lord will definitely lead you out of such mistakes.

Also, the enemy can only use lies against you if you are ignorant of the truth, or if it is their word against yours. In this case, you will not have any problem if everybody already knows that you are a truthful person. But in a case where they do not know that you are truthful, you simply need to be patient and continue to walk in truth.

When all you do is in truth, it will be easy for you to love your enemy because you know that they cannot use anything you do against you. You walk in the light.

Love Your Enemy

And Jesus came and spoke to them, saying, "All authority has been given to Me in heaven and on earth.
(Matthew 28:18)

And you are complete in Him, who is the head of all principality and power.
(Colossians 2:10)

Jesus is the head of all principality and power. He has all power in heaven and on earth. Every other power is subject to Him. He has the final say. Therefore, when you follow Him and do as He says in every area of your life, no other power in heaven and on earth can stand against you. You can only be afraid of your enemy's power when you are not doing what the Lord

Love Your Enemy (II)

tells you to or when you do not have revelation knowledge of the fact that He has all power.

The power of Christ is used in love. It is not used to show off or for selfish gain. It is not used in hatred. It is not used for retaliation or revenge. The power of Christ is used for establishing God's will. It is the will of God that love and truth should reign on the earth. Therefore, any power that is not used in truth and love is not of God or from God.

> *"But I say to you, love your enemies, bless those who curse you, do good to those who hate you, and pray for those who spitefully use you and persecute you."*
>
> **(Matthew 5:44)**

Love Your Enemy

The words of Jesus from the above scripture are clear. All these are possible when we know that we are in Christ; we are in Christ Jesus who told us to do this. Definitely, when we grow in Him, we grow in the understanding of why He told us to do these things.

You do not need to pray any bad prayers against your enemies, except to pray against the spiritual forces backing them. Every wicked person or someone that hates you is allowing the devil to work in their lives or through them. So you can pray against the work of the devil in their lives. Pray against the darkness in their heart. Pray against the powers backing them. Pray that they will come to know the truth in Christ Jesus. Pray that the love of God should enter or fill their heart. And you can also ask the Holy Spirit to help you with specific prayer points for them,

Love Your Enemy (II)

because it is possible that the people that hate you do so because of grief or loss, wrong ideology/philosophy or because they were abused, and so on. Your prayers for them can help them see the truth and cause them to make necessary changes that will make them better persons.

For example, if someone comes to you and says, "You will not see tomorrow," you do not need to reply the person with "It is you that will not see tomorrow." You can say, "I know I will see tomorrow," or "I will definitely see tomorrow because I know I can't die, I have eternal life in Christ Jesus." This way, you are establishing your authority in love.

Please note that if anyone says any negative words to you, you must respond right there and then with positive words, and do not say

Love Your Enemy

the negative words back to them. But if it is a situation where it will look like you are being disrespectful or insubordinate, you can wait till you leave the person's presence and then say the positive words over yourself without saying the negative words back to them. After God, it is only you that have the final say over your life.

In addition, you can also pray against your enemy's actions/wickedness/evil works without having any bit of hatred for them. In fact, it will seem like you are correcting them in love. For instance, a parent that restrains a child without spanking the child in order for the child to receive an injection at the hospital, the parent holds the child down encouraging him/her to receive the

> *It is the will of God that love and truth should reign on the earth.*

Love Your Enemy (II)

medicine. All the attempts of the child to break free are curbed by the parent. Similarly, you can use your authority in Christ to stop the evil acts of your enemy, praying for them to receive the truth and new life in Christ. And if God gives you the opportunity to actually stop the evil acts of your enemy, you do so still encouraging them to receive the truth and new life in Christ.

For example, Ahithophel's conspiracy against David: David prayed that the Lord should turn the counsel of Ahithophel into foolishness, and he also did what he could to defeat the counsel. You can read from 2 Samuel 15 to 2 Samuel 17 to know the full story, but let us see a few verses.

> ***Then Absalom sent for Ahithophel the Gilonite, David's counselor, from his city—from Giloh—while he offered***

sacrifices. And the conspiracy grew strong, for the people with Absalom continually increased in number. Then someone told David, saying, "Ahithophel is among the conspirators with Absalom." And David said, "O LORD, I pray, turn the counsel of Ahithophel into foolishness!" Now it happened when David had come to the top of the mountain, where he worshipped God—there was Hushai the Archite coming to meet him with his robe torn and dust on his head. David said to him, "If you go on with me, then you will become a burden to me. "But if you return to the city, and say to Absalom, 'I will be your servant,' then you may defeat the counsel of Ahithophel for me.

(2 Samuel 15:31-34)

Love Your Enemy (II)

So Absalom and all the men of Israel said, "The advice of Hushai the Archite is better than the advice of Ahithophel." For the LORD had purposed to defeat the good advice of Ahithophel, to the intent that the LORD might bring disaster on Absalom.

(2 Samuel 17:14)

Now when Ahithophel saw that his advice was not followed, he saddled a donkey, and arose and went home to his house, to his city. Then he put his household in order, and hanged himself, and died; and he was buried in his father's tomb.

(2 Samuel 17:23)

Love Your Enemy

David simply prayed that the LORD should turn the counsel of Ahithophel into foolishness, and he took a step against the counsel not Ahithophel. But in the end, Ahithophel hanged himself and died. Similarly, you do not need to pray against your enemy as a person, but you pray against their wickedness or evil works, and if you have the opportunity, you can take steps in righteousness to stop or curb the evil acts and leave the outcome on them to God.

Jesus is the way to God. He is the way to love. Without Jesus Christ, it is impossible to love your enemies genuinely. It is only in Jesus that you can have new life that is eternally blissful. You can accept Him into your life right now; accept the new life that He gives.

Love Your Enemy (II)

You can pray this prayer audibly:

Heavenly Father, I thank You for loving me dearly, I thank You for sending your son, Jesus, to this world to die for my salvation, and He resurrected the third day for my justification and righteousness in You. I receive new life in Christ Jesus; old things are passed away; all things are become new. Lord Jesus, I believe in You, I will follow you and do as you say, always. I am reborn in Christ. Thank You heavenly Father, thank you Lord, in Jesus' name, amen.

Love Your Enemy

I rejoice with you; you are now alive in Christ!

Your goal now is to grow in knowing Jesus. One good place to start is to read about Him in the bible. You can start reading from the gospels according to Matthew, Mark, Luke, and John in the new testament of the bible. And pray to Him to lead you to the church He wants you to fellowship. You are in for a wonderful time in Christ. You are blessed!

Chapter Five

YES, YOU CAN

Love Your Enemy

Yes, you can! Yes, you can love your enemies. Yes, you can do good to your enemies. You have what it takes in Christ. Do not be too concerned with having earthly possessions. Once you can place things in their rightful place or perspective, knowing that it is not a do or die affair to have anything, it will be easy for you to love your enemy because most of the time, if not all of the time, your enemy is your enemy because of earthly things.

> ***Do not love the world or the things in the world. If anyone loves the world, the love of the Father is not in him. For all that is in the world—the lust of the flesh, the lust of the eyes, and the pride of life—is not of the Father but is of the world.***

Yes, You Can

And the world is passing away, and the lust of it; but he who does the will of God abides forever.
(1 John 2:15-17)

When you continue doing the will of God, you abide forever. The world is passing away. What your enemy hates you for is passing away. They need to see this; little wonder you need to pray for them instead of hating them.

You need to be truthful, loving, hardworking, faithful, full of integrity, excellent in your duties, compassionate, patient, and perfect in your ways. So that no enemy will be able to use anything against you except they try to use outside factors or their own machinations against you, which the Lord will turn to naught.

Love Your Enemy

Instead of trying to get back at your enemy, try to improve on yourself. Make yourself better.

Daniel is an exceptionally good example for us.

It pleased Darius to set over the kingdom one hundred and twenty satraps, to be over the whole kingdom; And over these, three governors, of whom Daniel was one, that the satraps might give account to them, so that the king will suffer no loss. Then this Daniel distinguished himself above the governors and satraps, because an excellent spirit was in him; and the king gave thought to setting him over the whole realm.

Yes, You Can

So the governors and satraps sought to find some charge against Daniel concerning the kingdom; but they could find no charge or fault, because he was faithful; nor was any error or fault found in him. Then those men said, "We shall not find any charge against this Daniel unless we find it against him concerning the law of his God."

(Daniel 6:1-5)

Please, you can read the entire chapter six to see how God saved Daniel from the machinations of his enemies.

My emphasis is on the fact that they could not find any fault in Daniel because an excellent spirit was in him. You too, as long as you are in Christ,

Love Your Enemy

already have an excellent spirit in you, you just have to continue to walk and grow in the Spirit. In case you think you are not excellent or cannot achieve excellence, if you are in Christ, just start to walk or work towards excellence. Begin with the little things you can do. You can start with ensuring that your yes is yes, and your no is no. And little things you do like cleaning your room or house, do it excellently and keep growing until it is evident in every aspect of your life.

The decision for writing this book came after holding a couple of teaching programs on love your enemy. So at one of such events, precisely the one that was held at Campus Christian Fellowship (CCF-NIFES), Federal University of Technology Akure (FUTA), 13th August 2017. Someone made a contribution during the question-and-answer session that I would like to mention here. He said that he had always wondered why God allowed the youths that mocked Elisha to be mauled by the two female bears after Elisha pronounced a curse on them.

Then he went up from there to Bethel; and as he was going up the road, some youths came from the city and mocked him, and said to him, "Go up, you baldhead! Go up, you baldhead!" So he turned around and looked at them, and pronounced a curse on them in the name of the LORD. And two female bears came out of the woods and mauled forty-two of the youths.

(2 Kings 2:23-24)

Love Your Enemy

He continued that because of the teaching that day on *love your enemy* he can now see that Elisha was just starting to know God, so he did not know God's love yet. But after he spent time with God, he grew in God's love. He said that this must be the case because a few chapters after, Elisha counseled the king not to kill the army of his enemy but to make a feast for them and send them back to their master.

> ***Now when the king of Israel saw them, he said to Elisha, "My father, shall I kill them? Shall I kill them?" But he answered, "You shall not kill them. Would you kill those whom you have taken captive with your sword and your bow? Set food and water before them, that they may eat and drink and go to their master."***

Yes, You Can

Then he prepared a great feast for them; and after they ate and drank, he sent them away and they went to their master. So the bands of Syrian raiders came no more into the land of Israel.

(2 Kings 6:21-23)

Please, you can read the entire chapter six to know the full story.

So, I would like to put it to you that your maturity in God is a function of how much of God's love you have grown in and how much of it you give.

Finally, do not stop doing good for whatever reason. The least you can do is to try to look for a better way to continue the good you are

Love Your Enemy

doing. For example, if you have someone you are supporting financially so that he can buy food for his family, and you later find out that he was diverting most of the money into doing something irresponsible. Do not stop the financial support because of his irresponsibility, but rather look for another way to continue giving to him and his family. You could buy the food stuff yourself and send it to his family instead of giving him cash. This might cost you more, but it is worth it. Never allow someone's misdeed to stop you from doing good. You learn, you become wiser, and you think of better ways to continue. I cannot overstress this because this is one of the reasons there is little goodness in the society. If you must stop any good deed, let it be because you want to do something better, or because you no longer have the means to do it.

Yes, You Can

Remain in the goodness of God's love. And keep growing in God's love.

ABOUT THE AUTHOR

*O*luseye S. Olayiwola was born-again and received the baptism of the HOLY SPIRIT as a young teenager on Jan 14, 1996, at Rhema Chapel International Churches Surulere, Lagos. Since then his relationship with The LORD has been by the HOLY SPIRIT. He is happily married. His greatest passion is to continually love GOD and to do exactly what GOD says. He is an anointed teacher of God's Word and a minister of the gospel.

For enquiries, please email:
loveyourenemyoluseye@gmail.com

Printed in Great Britain
by Amazon